Contents

KT-409-821

Introduction

Amphetamines, which are powerful **stimulants**, have been around for more than a century and have been abused for nearly as long. They were developed as a medical treatment for all sorts of conditions but, one by one, these medical claims have been either disproved or shown to be greatly exaggerated. What has lingered, however, is the reputation that amphetamines quickly attained as a drug that could produce a sudden rush of energy, coupled with a sense that the user can do no wrong.

A suitable nickname

It is not surprising that such a drug earned the nickname 'speed', since users of the drug seem to operate at high speed. Constantly fidgeting, moving about and talking fifteen to the dozen, these users really do seem to be operating in a higher gear. The truth, however, is different and quite disturbing. Nothing in life comes free and this 'extra' energy is no exception. The boost of energy that amphetamines seem to give is really borrowed from the body's own reserves, and there is a price to pay.

The immediate price is the sense of depression and **lethargy** that comes when the drug wears off. This is when the body needs to recharge, having been running on empty for hours on end. During the 'high', however, the body has been strained in many ways that are potentially harmful: with the increased energy come increased breathing, heart rate and blood pressure. The user can simply overheat or run into complications related to existing health problems.

Dicing with death

In the longer term, users of amphetamines need to take more and more of the drug to get 'high', or sometimes simply to feel 'normal'.

Need to Know

Amphetamines

Sean Connolly

Heinemann

www.heinemann.co.uk
visit our website to find out more information about **Heinemann Lib**

To order:
☎ Phone 44 (0) 1865 888066
📠 Send a fax to 44 (0) 1865 314091
💻 Visit the Heinemann Bookshop at www.heinemann.co.uk to browse our catalogue and order online.

First published in Great Britain by Heinemann Library, Halley Court, Jordan Hill, Oxford OX2 8EJ, a division of
Reed Educational and Professional Publishing Ltd.

Heinemann is a registered trademark of Reed Educational & Professional Publishing Limited.

Oxford Melbourne Auckland Johannesburg Blantyre Gaborone Ibadan Portsmouth NH (USA) Chicago

© Reed Educational and Professional Publishing Ltd 2000
The moral right of the proprietor has been asserted.

Designed by M2 Graphic Design
Printed in Hong Kong / China
Originated by Ambassador Litho Ltd.

ISBN 0431 097771 (hardback)   ISBN 0431 097879 (paperback)
04 03 02 01   05 04 03 02 01
10 9 8 7 6 5 4 3 2   10 9 8 7 6 5 4 3 2 1

British Library Cataloguing in Publication Data
Sean Connolly
Amphetamines – (Need to know)
1. Amphetamines – Juvenile literature 2. Amphetamine abuse – Juvenile literature I Title 362.2'98

Acknowledgements
The Publishers would like to thank the following for permission to reproduce photographs:
Allsport: Vandystadt pg.39; Bubbles: pg.29, pg.50, pg.51, Pauline Cutter pg.43; Camera Press: pg.30;
Corbis: pg.21, pg.33, pg.45; Gareth Boden: pg.26; Hulton Getty: pg.17, pg.18, pg.35; Images Colour
Library: pg.10; Impact: James Fraser pg.23, Barnard pg.25, Piers Cavendish pg.32; Network: Jonathan
Olley pg. 31; Photofusion: pg.46, Clarissa Leahy pg.11, Julia Martin pg.15, Mark Campbell pg.22, Crispin
Hughes pg.48; Police Forensic Department: pg.5, pg.6, pg.7, pg.41; Rex Features: pg.8, pg.38, Steve
Woods pg.36; Science Photo Library: pg.13; Tony Stone: pg.9.

Cover photograph reproduced with permission of Science Photo Library.

Every effort has been made to contact copyright holders of any material reproduced in this book. Any omis-
sions will be rectified in subsequent printings if notice is given to the publisher.

Any words appearing in the text in bold, **like this**, are explained in the Glossary.

A single dose of powdered amphetamine is often folded in paper and known as a 'wrap'.

This problem of **dependence** is typical of many drugs and, at the very least, long-term amphetamine users run the risk of developing an expensive habit. More importantly, though, they face far graver health risks, culminating in possible death from overdose or (when the drug is **injected**) infection from the **HIV** virus. These risks underline the health-awareness slogan 'Speed kills' – originally used for driving but widened to warn about the dangers of amphetamines ('speed').

What are amphetamines?

Amphetamines are substances that act as **stimulants** on the body's central nervous system. They enter the bloodstream very quickly and then arouse the user in the same way that naturally produced **adrenaline** does. This effect, like that of adrenaline, has often been compared to the 'fight or flight' impulse. What adrenaline does – and what amphetamines mimic – is to increase the heartbeat and blood pressure, **dilate** the body's breathing tubes, increase blood sugar levels and prepare the body for an emergency.

Most amphetamines are sold in powdered form known chemically as amphetamine sulphate.

Such a combination – a normal defence when someone is fearful or attacked – acts as part of the 'buzz' for someone who is taking amphetamines **recreationally**.

On the streets, this drug is available mainly as an off-white powder known as amphetamine sulphate, which is also known by a number of slang terms, including 'speed', 'whizz', 'billy' and 'phets'. The powder is usually doctored with similar-coloured powders such as talc, paracetamol and even **strychnine** – together, these other substances can comprise more than 90 per cent of what is sold as amphetamines. This type of amphetamine can be **snorted**, dabbed from the finger to the mouth, mixed with a drink or **injected**. 'Base' amphetamine is a sticky paste that comes from earlier on in the production process and is usually about three to five times purer than amphetamine sulphate.

The amphetamine 'high'

Depending on the user's **tolerance** to amphetamines, and the purity of the drug itself, these effects begin to take place about half an hour after it is taken. The user begins to feel more energetic, alert and talkative, then experiences a loss in appetite and begins to breathe faster.

People report feeling more confident, losing any sense of self-criticism. This altered state lasts from four to six hours. The 'high' produced by amphetamines also leads to a corresponding 'low' when the effects wear off, and users feel tired and irritable for a few days after taking the drug.

Some amphetamine users, aiming for a more intense high, take a smokeable form of amphetamine known as 'ice', although this type of amphetamine is quite rare. Its effects last up to 39 hours and it is thought to be one of the most highly addictive drugs in the world.

❝Faster, faster, until the thrill of speed overcomes the fear of death.❞

(Hunter S. Thompson, author and past user of amphetamines, writing about speed in both senses)

What's the attraction?

There are many reasons why people are attracted to amphetamines. In addition to the usual reasons for beginning to take a drug, such as **peer pressure**, other factors make some people think that life will be better once they try amphetamines. Young people hear stories about how much energy people have while they are high, and how this energy and self-confidence help them cope with problems or simply enjoy life on a higher plane. Others, while noting these factors, are attracted by the way amphetamines burn off calories and reduce appetite – this weight-loss aspect is what led to the legal use of amphetamines in the first place.

Amphetamines became one of the drugs associated with the 'rave culture' that developed in the 1980s. Some party-goers were lured by the promise of being able to stay awake for hours on end and having a prolonged boost of energy.

An extra edge

In addition to these pleasure-related reasons for taking amphetamines, there are others more closely linked to jobs or outside interests. Many fashion models speak of being encouraged to take **stimulants** to keep their weight down, or to cope with the irregular hours and constant travelling involved with the job. Some people involved in certain sports, such as judo and shooting, believe the heightened awareness will help them concentrate.

What goes up...

There is a price to pay for all this 'free' energy that amphetamines seem to offer. In the short term, even while buzzing with extra energy, the user's body is working overtime. The increased heartbeat and blood pressure can pose an immediate threat of heart disease and even stroke, in part because amphetamines have led to heart **palpitations** and have caused tiny blood vessels elsewhere to rupture or block. When these blood vessels burst they leave red spots, which are visible on the faces of some amphetamine users. If blood vessels burst in the brain then the user runs the risk of paralysis or coma. Other side-effects can occur while the drug is taking effect, including diarrhoea, a foul taste in the mouth, sweating and an increased need to urinate.

Mixing amphetamines with other drugs is like playing Russian roulette. Taking amphetamines with LSD, for example, can cause **hallucinations** and **paranoia**. Taking amphetamines and ecstasy together – a combination that often occurs at raves – is dangerous because both drugs make the heart beat faster. This places a strain on the heart and increases the likelihood of dehydration and overheating.

Some people involved in quick reflex sports such as judo are tempted to take amphetamines because they believe the drug increases awareness and concentration.

What's the attraction?

...must come down

The after-effects of amphetamine use are as dramatic as the high the drug provides. As the initial effects of the drug wear off, the user begins to 'come down' quite dramatically. The 'extra' energy that amphetamines supply is actually provided by the body's own energy reserves, which means that the user will feel tired and rundown for a few days after using the drug. Amphetamines simply postpone the need for rest and food rather than replacing it. With this feeling of tiredness, many people also feel irritable, restless and anxious.

Longer-term effects are also worrying. Regular users who take high doses may develop delusions, **hallucinations** and feelings of **paranoia**. In some cases, users have been diagnosed as being mentally ill, taking months to make a full recovery – if at all. Part of this mental health problem stems from what researchers believe is damage caused to **neurons** in the brain. No one knows for sure whether they regain their normal function when amphetamine use stops.

Many women who use amphetamines regularly find that their periods become irregular or even stop. In addition, those women who take the contraceptive pill run serious risk of high blood pressure because – like the combination of amphetamines and ecstasy – both chemicals increase the heart rate.

Across society

Amphetamines are possibly the second most popular illegal drug in the UK, after cannabis. They are widely available in their various forms and the cost – about £10 for a gram – is within the reach of most people. Some people are tempted to use the drug as an occasional 'one-off', perhaps to stay up all night to write an essay or to complete a job. Others are drawn by nostalgia – a 'retro' taste either for the American writers of the **Beat Generation** of the 1950s or for the days of the Mods in Britain in the 1960s. Both groups led wild lives which were fuelled by amphetamines (see pages 20–21).

Coupled with the **prevalence** and relatively low cost of the drug is the way in which it regularly features in large gatherings such as pop festivals, raves and similar venues. Both the drug itself and the exaggerated claims made on its behalf, spread quickly through an impressionable crowd.

Are amphetamines addictive?

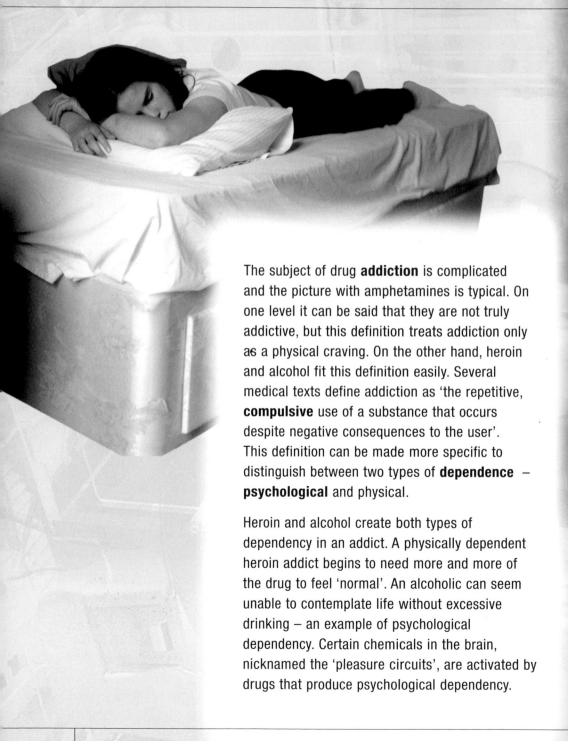

The subject of drug **addiction** is complicated and the picture with amphetamines is typical. On one level it can be said that they are not truly addictive, but this definition treats addiction only as a physical craving. On the other hand, heroin and alcohol fit this definition easily. Several medical texts define addiction as 'the repetitive, **compulsive** use of a substance that occurs despite negative consequences to the user'. This definition can be made more specific to distinguish between two types of **dependence** – **psychological** and physical.

Heroin and alcohol create both types of dependency in an addict. A physically dependent heroin addict begins to need more and more of the drug to feel 'normal'. An alcoholic can seem unable to contemplate life without excessive drinking – an example of psychological dependency. Certain chemicals in the brain, nicknamed the 'pleasure circuits', are activated by drugs that produce psychological dependency.

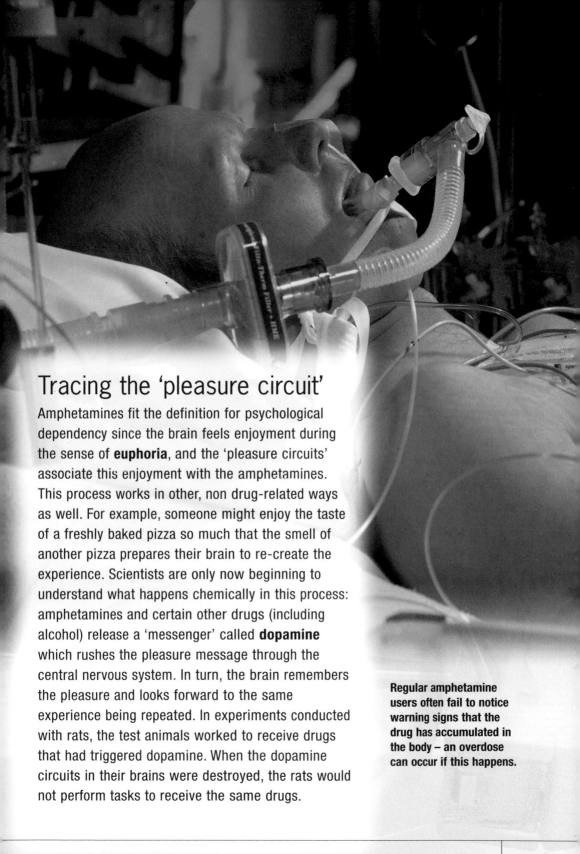

Tracing the 'pleasure circuit'

Amphetamines fit the definition for psychological dependency since the brain feels enjoyment during the sense of **euphoria**, and the 'pleasure circuits' associate this enjoyment with the amphetamines. This process works in other, non drug-related ways as well. For example, someone might enjoy the taste of a freshly baked pizza so much that the smell of another pizza prepares their brain to re-create the experience. Scientists are only now beginning to understand what happens chemically in this process: amphetamines and certain other drugs (including alcohol) release a 'messenger' called **dopamine** which rushes the pleasure message through the central nervous system. In turn, the brain remembers the pleasure and looks forward to the same experience being repeated. In experiments conducted with rats, the test animals worked to receive drugs that had triggered dopamine. When the dopamine circuits in their brains were destroyed, the rats would not perform tasks to receive the same drugs.

Regular amphetamine users often fail to notice warning signs that the drug has accumulated in the body – an overdose can occur if this happens.

Are amphetamines addictive?

The physical side

Even the physical definition of **dependency**, which amphetamines don't meet in the strictest definition, is a bit ambiguous. It is true that the body never acquires the intense craving that is typical of physical dependence on, for example, heroin. However, amphetamine use does share an important quality with addictions to drugs that do promote physical dependence – this quality is known as **tolerance**.

Basically, tolerance refers to the increasing amount of a drug that someone needs to achieve the same 'high'. Alcohol is a good example. One or two pints of lager would make a first-time drinker quite drunk, while a regular adult drinker would probably need four or five pints to reach the same state. Amphetamine users quickly develop a tolerance for the drug, needing more – or purer – amounts of it to get that same 'rush' that they first experienced.

Linked to the idea of physical dependency is the concept of **withdrawal** – symptoms of ill health that occur when an addict stops using a drug. At its most extreme – in coming off heroin the process is known as 'cold turkey' – it is deeply unsettling both mentally and physically. Amphetamines, taken in small regular doses, do not produce this effect. However, since increased tolerance promotes the use of ever-increasing amounts, the user runs the risk of developing a range of **psychological** problems after stopping. These range from delusions and **hallucinations** to cases of **paranoid psychosis**, from which it might take months to recover. Sometimes the condition is irreversible.

Upper limits

The increased amounts of the drug taken by many amphetamine users imposes a range of other problems, not all of which are truly **addictive** but are definite byproducts of the psychological dependence. These side-effects include damaged blood vessels and heart failure as well as liver problems. Overall, because of the long-term energy demands produced by the drug, users will develop **deficiencies** in vitamins and calcium, leaving them more exposed to infection. The most serious problem about ever-increasing use of amphetamines is, quite simply, that it can be fatal. It is easy to overdose on amphetamines – and overdoses are often fatal.

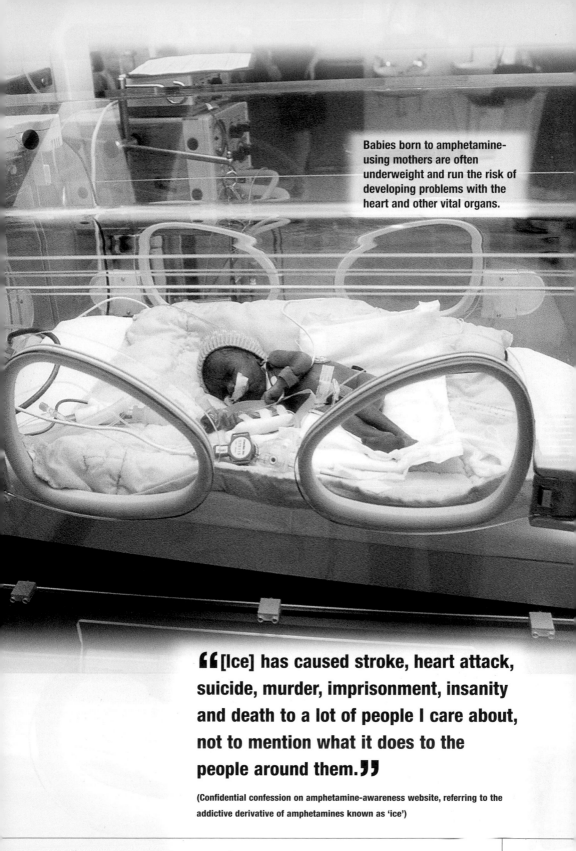

Babies born to amphetamine-using mothers are often underweight and run the risk of developing problems with the heart and other vital organs.

❝[Ice] has caused stroke, heart attack, suicide, murder, imprisonment, insanity and death to a lot of people I care about, not to mention what it does to the people around them.❞

(Confidential confession on amphetamine-awareness website, referring to the addictive derivative of amphetamines known as 'ice')

A cure-all is born

Amphetamines were first **synthesized** in Germany in 1887 but it was only in the 1920s that they were first tested on humans. It became clear at once that these were powerful drugs that caused the body to respond as if it were facing an emergency. Such effects suggested that there was medical potential in producing quantities of the drug, and subsequent tests concentrated on this **pharmaceutical** development.

At about the same time in the 1920s, a number of naturally occurring drugs were shown to act as successful treatments of asthma and other ailments. One of these drugs, ephedrine, was particularly successful but it had to be extracted from plants which were in short supply. In 1927 a pharmaceutical chemist called Gordon Alles synthesized amphetamines which resembled ephedrine. His research opened the door for widespread production – and prescription – of amphetamines by the medical establishment.

A potential cure-all

Benzedrine, which is a **trade-name** of this type of synthesized amphetamine, appeared on the market in the 1930s. In addition to its role in treating asthma – which had sparked the research in the first place – it was accepted as an effective treatment for depression, **narcolepsy**, opium **addiction** and even seasickness. Amphetamines were also sold, without the need for a prescription, as nasal decongestants in the form of spray inhalers.

While many people in the 1930s experienced relief from illnesses and painful conditions thanks to the use of amphetamines, other people began using amphetamines for pleasure. Initially this type of use spread by word of mouth. Relieved asthma sufferers, while telling of the immediate breathing relief, also spoke of the sense of **euphoria** that accompanied the drug's medical effects. The availability of amphetamines in inhaler form made them readily accessible, affordable and simple to use.

Wartime spread

The **Second World War**, which took place mainly in the early 1940s, imposed immense strains on the nations involved. Millions of people had to fight and newsreel films of the battles made the cost of war even more vivid in people's minds.

Governments on both sides of this conflict used amphetamines in huge quantities to build fighting spirit. Soldiers in all fighting forces – especially British, Japanese and American – were given millions of amphetamine pills to boost morale and to combat battle fatigue.

Speed at war

Records indicate that some 72 million amphetamine tablets were distributed among British fighting forces alone during the Second World War. Kamikaze pilots, the much-feared Japanese 'suicide bombers', also used amphetamines to boost the '**samurai**' spirit. Adolph Hitler, leader of Nazi Germany during the war, was **injected** with a powerful amphetamine up to five times a day throughout the war.

A cure-all is born

Spreading the word

When the war ended, the reputation of amphetamines had been thoroughly established and was spread to many parts of the world. Soldiers returning to the United States and Great Britain recalled their effectiveness. In many cases, though, the same soldiers had begun showing signs of **addiction**. With millions of pills having been so recently supplied it was not surprising that amphetamines were easily available for anyone who wanted to continue using them, or who was curious about their 'miracle effects'.

In the years immediately following the **Second World War** amphetamines became a way of life for many lorry drivers, university students and others who needed to prolong the time during which they could stay awake and alert. Using amphetamines for pleasure was becoming more common in the West. The story was similar in Japan, where millions of surplus American amphetamine tablets were simply dumped on the Japanese market. **Recreational** use of amphetamines also became common there.

The real boom

While amphetamines were establishing themselves as a drug of choice among many recreational users, there was also a huge surge in their medical use. During the 1950s and 1960s they were prescribed widely for fatigue, depression and as slimming aids. It seemed that people couldn't get enough of this drug. In 1958 alone, some 3.5 billion tablets were produced in the United States, enough to supply every American man, woman and child with 20 standard (5–15 mg) doses. The picture was similar in Britain. In 1961, for example, amphetamines accounted for 2.5 per cent of all National Health Service prescriptions.

These trends continued, with more and more people becoming convinced that amphetamines were the answer to their problems. Legal production in the United States rose to 12 billion tablets in 1971, and much of this total was diverted to the illegal market. The US and UK governments then imposed **quotas** on production and regulated prescriptions more closely. By that time it was becoming clear that for medical purposes, amphetamines were at worst ineffective and at best inferior to other, safer treatments.

Speed cultures

By the 1950s amphetamines, by now known widely as 'speed' on both sides of the Atlantic, were part of the illegal drug landscape. The inhalers that had done so much to increase the popularity of amphetamines in the 1930s were gone and the drugs were now taken mainly in pill form. By the early 1960s other illegal drugs such as cannabis and LSD were beginning to appear, but amphetamines retained their own popularity.

The Swinging Sixties

It was in Britain in the 1960s that amphetamines regained a high profile. 'Swinging London' was the heart of a booming fashion and music world and young people followed changing trends closely. One group of smartly dressed young people, known as the Mods, sped around on motor scooters while they looked for 'action'. Mods took amphetamines regularly in order to stay awake in the all-night clubs of London, Liverpool, Manchester and other British cities. Despite UK **legislation** in 1964, making amphetamines harder to obtain, Mods never seemed to run short of 'speed'.

Another group of British drug users began to match the amphetamine use of the Mods. **Intravenous** users of heroin and cocaine began **injecting** amphetamines in 1967 after some doctors began describing the drug as a safer alternative to cocaine. The UK Ministry of Health did not approve of this move, and ensured that quantities of injectable amphetamines were confined to hospital pharmacies.

The Beats

One of the first, and most important, blossomings of youth culture arrived with the '**Beat Generation**' of the 1950s. The 'Beats' were a group of writers and artists who rejected what they saw as the stuffiness of the world around them. Perhaps their most famous member was the American author Jack Kerouac, whose novel *On the Road* told of their adventures in search of thrills and excitement. The Beats were no strangers to drugs. It was said that Kerouac typed his novel in one furious session, keeping himself awake for hours on end with amphetamines. Whether or not this is true, many young people of the 1950s and early 1960s believed the story, and felt that amphetamines could fuel their own rebellious spirit.

The author Jack Kerouac, who it is alleged used amphetamines to remain awake while working.

Who takes amphetamines?

In keeping with their original development as medicines, amphetamines still have a number of accepted medical uses. The most important of these is in treating **Attention Deficit Disorder** in children. Amphetamines produce a distinct improvement in about three-quarters of these hyperactive children. It is curious that a drug that makes most people more active has this effect, but children receiving this treatment show marked improvement. They also feel few of the pleasant effects of amphetamines such as feelings of **euphoria**. Amphetamines are also used to treat the disorder known as **narcolepsy**. The main symptoms of this condition are sudden, uncontrollable attacks of sleepiness.

Most other medical claims for amphetamines have been abandoned. They are no longer widely used to treat depression. Amphetamines are still sometimes prescribed as diet pills, but this practice is declining because the negative side-effects outweigh any weight loss – which is usually short-term anyway.

The illegal scene

The illegal use of amphetamines seemed to decline after their last 'golden age' in the 1960s and early 1970s, as there were no obvious drug-taking successors to the Mods. This trend began to reverse itself in the late 1980s, however, as dance culture began to grow. Young people found themselves exposed to a wide variety of drugs, notably ecstasy and LSD. Amphetamines also became part of this scene because of the boost they gave.

Another reason for the resurgence of amphetamines – certainly within the rave culture – was that street ecstasy became less pure. Amphetamines seemed to offer a better alternative for staying up long hours. Serious users of amphetamines also found that, unlike ecstasy, impure amphetamines could be **injected** to maximize their effect. Injecting amphetamines leads to increased use of the drug, since the drug user very quickly builds up **tolerance** to it and needs to take more to achieve the same effect.

A wide base

Despite the popularity of ecstasy, amphetamines still seem to be the most popular illegal drug in the UK, after cannabis. A series of surveys conducted in the early 1990s confirmed this. Around ten per cent of respondents in the 15–29 age group claimed to have tried the drug at least once.

A similar figure of about one in ten who came to drug **rehabilitation** centres said that amphetamines were the main drug that they used. More than half of this second group were **injecting** the drug, the second largest percentage of injectors after heroin users.

Amphetamine use is now part of a drugs scene that is much more complicated than it was two or three decades ago. People are using the drugs together with other drugs – often with serious side-effects – and the amphetamines themselves are being taken in a variety of forms. The high figure of injectors (noted above) indicates one departure from the 'traditional' sniffing or pill-popping image of amphetamine users. More concentrated forms of amphetamines, such as 'meth' (see panel, page 28), also tempt users who are looking for a more dramatic high.

Using amphetamines

A regular user of amphetamines usually wakes up feeling very tired – sleep is delayed by the drug and then the body feels the need to pay back the energy used while the drug took its effect. The day drags by slowly, especially when compared with the rush of the night before, and the user feels depressed and distracted. If it's a Saturday, the amphetamine user will be counting the hours to the evening when there will be another chance to take the drug and feel 'normal' once again.

The afternoon crawls by and the amphetamine user might try to escape the uncomfortable feelings of moodiness and itchiness on the skin – a typical side-effect of amphetamine use – by taking some glucose drink or fruit juice. These help to replace the sugar used up by the extra energy 'borrowed' by amphetamines but, to have any real benefit, these drinks should be taken while the drug is working.

In the evening, perhaps half an hour before a rave, the amphetamine user might join others to **snort** or dab some amphetamine sulphate on their tongues. Within 30 minutes the previous night's sense of **euphoria** has returned. The user will be babbling away and dancing for hours on end. By the time the drug has worn off, in the early hours of the morning, it will be hard to fall asleep. When sleep does come, it seems to be not nearly refreshing enough. The user wakes up the next day feeling very down again – completing the cycle of borrowing energy and paying for it afterwards.

The pressure of work – including schoolwork – lures some people into taking amphetamines in the search for extra energy.

'Scoring' amphetamines

Amphetamines, and the various derivatives of it such as 'meth' (see panel, page 28), are widely available in the UK and in the United States. They seep into the **black market** either through theft of legally prepared amounts or by production in illegal laboratories. People involved in any drug scene – whether cannabis, ecstasy, LSD or cocaine – become exposed to it and are aware of its availability. Unlike some other illegal drugs such as cannabis or heroin, amphetamines often originate in the country of sale. The comparative lack of risk in getting the substance through Customs means that it is relatively inexpensive and plentiful. All of these factors mean that is very easy to 'score' (get hold of) amphetamines, even if the buyer can never be sure of the quality.

Word of mouth

As with so many other drugs, amphetamines have a reputation that goes before them. People who are otherwise disinclined to take drugs are often told that speed is a safe way to feel great and enjoy life at a higher pitch. Typically, the side-effects are ignored or glossed over in these accounts. Many users of amphetamines first take the drug at a rave or other large-scale venue, when amphetamines seem to be the cheapest and least dangerous way of enjoying the dance experience more fully.

As well as being used occasionally by people who are not typical drug-users, amphetamines are often specifically chosen by those who are seriously involved with drugs. Users of cocaine, worried about its high cost, often turn to amphetamines because the 'high' is similar and lasts longer. Many people who **inject** drugs such as heroin turn to amphetamines because of the serious concerns about heroin **addiction**.

Family and friends

Regularly taking any illegal drug – or even some legal drugs such as alcohol – produces a marked effect on the way a person deals with their family and friends. To a parent or sibling who is aware of the effects of amphetamines, there would be some tell-tale signs that a family member was a regular user. Apart from some physical signals such as weight-loss and itching, they would notice some differences in behaviour. Some of these behavioural changes might be harder to pinpoint, since they are often exaggerated traits of a young person's normal character.

'Scoring' amphetamines

Early morning grogginess and irritability – in themselves fairly common among teenagers – seem more profound. Linked to this would be a new pattern of late nights and lessened appetite. It might take more dramatic symptoms – indicative of fairly heavy amphetamine use – for some family members to realize that something was wrong. Witnessing a constant sense of panic or **paranoia** in a loved one is alarming, even if you don't know that it is caused by drug abuse.

Friends are often in a better position to identify the reasons for an amphetamine user's changed character. Most young people are highly tuned to attitudes of other young people, and quickly realize when a friend has begun showing less interest in them or has taken up with a new group. Another important reason why friends are more likely to get to the root of the problem – there is a good chance they will see an amphetamine user on a high. While the drug is in full flow, outsiders can identify uncharacteristic displays of boastfulness, urgency or excessive talking.

The drug user's friends are often placed in the awkward position of trying to decide between maintaining their friendship by keeping quiet, or taking the harder decision to try to warn them of the risks they run.

Methamphetamines

Methyl amphetamines, usually known as methamphetamines or simply 'meth', are a powerful **compound** of amphetamines. They are similar in effect and consequences to amphetamines but slightly more powerful. However, there is one dramatic difference. Meth can be converted to a concentrated, crystallized **freebase** form, known as 'ice', which can be smoked or injected. This form of meth creates disturbing **auditory hallucinations**, severe paranoia and violent behaviour. The effects last longer than with normal amphetamines and the crash after coming down off the drug is more severe than with amphetamines or cocaine. Meth, and in particular 'ice', can become extremely **addictive**. It is far more common in the United States than in Britain.

"Lots of people I know take speed. They buy it round the corner from where I live and share it. My boyfriend says it's a really fun drug to take."

(Louise, 13)

"My friend's sister said she took speed to lose weight. She lost about two stone really quickly."

(Lisa, 13)

Price and prevalence

The most common form of **'recreational'** amphetamines is amphetamine sulphate, which is the white crystalline substance that most users **snort**, or sniff up their noses. The sulphate costs around £5–10 for a 'wrap', a single portion sold wrapped in small folded bits of paper. The price of a wrap has remained about the same for more than a decade unlike escalating prices of some other illegal drugs – which means that amphetamines are now considered a 'cheap high'.

Set routines

Many users follow a snorting ritual, using a rolled-up banknote as a tube to inhale the drug. One regular user, quoted in a drug survey, said, 'It feels sharp and **acrid** in the nose when snorted, and it doesn't give the easy **exhilaration** of cocaine. It just makes my heart pound as everything becomes fast and urgent.' Others prefer to rub the drug against their gums, which is said to indicate how pure the amphetamine is by the level of tingling it causes. A wrap contains about half a gram of drugs, of which only about 25 mg (five per cent) is pure amphetamines. It is the lack of purity of this type of amphetamines – as noted earlier – that leads some users to **inject** the drug, to maximize its effects by putting it straight into the bloodstream. This has many potentially serious – even fatal – side-effects if users share needles. There is a risk of infection with **HIV**, hepatitis and other diseases.

Amphetamine varieties

Instead of injecting amphetamine
sulphate, some users turn to more
concentrated – and more expensive –
forms of amphetamines to get a
stronger 'high'. The most common of
these is 'meth' (see panel, page 28).
Others, along with their more
commonly used nicknames include:
dexamphetamine ('dexies'),
methylphenidate ('Rit'), and
durophet ('black bombers').

**❝I want to try speed.
I've heard it gives you
loads of energy and
has no side-effects.❞**

(Tom, 12)

The amphetamine industry

The amphetamines that appear in the drugs scene come from a number of different sources, many of which are large-scale producers. This stems from the long history that amphetamines had as legitimate medical drugs – a position that has been severely challenged in recent decades. Widespread production over many years, however, led to a number of developments that combined to make distribution of amphetamines very easy. Today's **black market** in amphetamines can be traced to these legitimate sources.

Noble origins

When, in Germany in the 1880s, amphetamines were first **synthesized** and their effects noted, they were considered safe **stimulants**. They were promoted as tonics which would aid physical wellbeing. At that time it was not uncommon to make grand claims about the effectiveness of a drug. Many popular drinks were sold largely on the basis of their health-restoring potential, for example, Coca-Cola, which was developed at around the same time, was sold as a pick-me-up. For many years its notoriously secret formula actually contained traces of the drug cocaine – reflected in the brand name. Amphetamines, and the products associated with them, were part of this trend and production was stepped up accordingly.

In some ways, these high-blown marketing claims about the merits of amphetamines were accurate. People *did* report feeling better in the short term and seemed to be able to perform certain tasks with more energy and enthusiasm. Problems of **dependence** and **tolerance** were either not noticed or simply ignored as companies made large profits from the drug.

The 'golden age' of **pharmaceutical** amphetamines – roughly from the 1930s to the 1960s – established the drug both in people's minds and in the industrial world. New manufacturing centres opened to meet the increasing demand. The millions of amphetamine tablets produced annually in the 1930s grew to billions before limits were placed on production in the early 1970s.

Modern variety

The 'golden age' of widespread medical amphetamine prescriptions is over. One by one the perceived benefits of the drug have either been disproved or they have been shown to be outweighed by the problems caused, such as the physical side-effects and dependence. Despite the strict regulations on amphetamines that apply in most countries (which even include strict penalties for non-prescription possession of the drug), amphetamines are still available in large quantities.

In 1960, police poured 15,000 amphetamine pills into an incinerator in Pennsylvania, USA. The pills were being supplied to truckers by service station attendants.

The amphetamine industry

Some of this supply comes from illegally diverting legally produced amphetamines – in effect, stealing it from the companies that manufacture it. Most of the amphetamines available on the street, however, are made in illegal laboratories.

'Virtual' amphetamines

The word amphetamines, although a mouthful in itself, is actually an **acronym** for a much longer term – **a**lpha-**m**ethyl-**phe**ne-thyl-**amine** – which is the proper chemical term for the drug. Despite its daunting scientific name, once they know its formula amateur chemists are able to **synthesize** amphetamines, provided they have some essential (inexpensive) basic ingredients.

In the 1960s, when illegal use of amphetamines reached its first peak, unofficial laboratories produced amphetamines in isolation from each other. Formulae and other information passed through an underground network, but there was little real contact among producers. This position has now changed. Internet websites are devoted to passing on information about producing amphetamines and other drugs, and underground chemists post the most detailed information about new varieties and methods to use. These 'virtual recipes' have brought amphetamine production to a much wider audience, and supplies have increased as a result.

Powering the powerful

It is hard now to realize that in the past a drug as potentially dangerous as amphetamines had the seal of approval of so many people, including world leaders. Nazi Germany's leader Adolph Hitler had **injections** of amphetamines regularly throughout the **Second World War**. He wasn't alone. About ten years later, during a major international conflict known as the Suez Crisis, UK Prime Minister Anthony Eden said he was 'living on Benzedrine' (a type of amphetamine).

A fine line

Websites providing information about production of amphetamines must ensure that they don't seem to be providing illegal information, even if they are. They use get-out clauses known as disclaimers at the beginning of each site, claiming that the material on the site is for information only. The following is part of just such a disclaimer:

'Some of the articles contained herein describe illegal activities, which may not be clearly identified as illegal. It is not recommended that any of the activities described herein actually be carried out.' This is followed by a series of articles with intricate step-by-step instructions on just how to perfect amphetamine production.

The cost of dependence

Despite widespread awareness of the dangers of **tolerance** and **psychological dependence** on amphetamines, the drug still maintains a deceptive reputation as a safe alternative to more seriously damaging drugs such as heroin and morphine. Amphetamines are often used by regular users of those other drugs, sometimes simply as a change but often as a means of weaning themselves off their **addiction** to the other drug. It is hard to gauge how effective this tactic is – if it is at all. Medical professionals warn that mixing amphetamines with *any* other drug has potentially serious side-effects, because of the combination of effects the drugs have on the body. Also, many people find themselves in a spiral of **cross-dependence**, where they need both the original drug of addiction and the amphetamines taken to offset that addiction.

Tainted glamour

Another realm in which the use of amphetamines has almost reached industrial proportions is the fashion industry. The fast-paced world of modelling, with its irregular hours and long-distance travel, leaves many people tempted to take **stimulants** to help them cope. Amphetamine use, although denied in many quarters, is said to be very common, with large amounts of the models' hefty fees being spent on amphetamines and other 'uppers'.

The frantic pace is not the only reason underlying the link between modelling and amphetamines. In recent years, fashion designers and the all-important fashion critics have become obsessed with what has been described as 'heroin chic'. There has been a trend for models to become ultra-thin, with a washed-out look that suggests regular drug use. While outright heroin use would produce this effect, it would be hard for a model to function professionally while taking heroin regularly. Amphetamines, however, have the reputation of burning away calories and leaving the user looking far thinner. A regular amphetamine user, whose body had been borrowing energy to burn away unwanted weight, would certainly fit this 'heroin chic' ideal. She might be anxious, depressed and irritable but she could still function. What happens after her modelling career ends is her own problem.

Speed can kill

In addition to the legitimate and **black market** production of amphetamines, a third industry is associated with the drug – the health industry. In social terms, the involvement of the medical profession is extremely costly as hard-pressed doctors, nurses, paramedics and health practitioners deal with the consequences of amphetamine use.

Drug-awareness campaigns on both sides of the Atlantic have recognized the enduring appeal of amphetamines, or 'speed'. By the mid-1960s the slogan 'Speed kills' became an effective link between the obvious dangers of reckless driving and what were then the less obvious side-effects of regular amphetamine use.

Public health

A tragic incident in July 1967 highlighted the concerns about amphetamines. During the gruelling Tour de France cycling race, Britain's leading cyclist, Tommy Simpson, collapsed unconscious by the roadside. He was flown to a nearby hospital in Avignon, but was dead on arrival. Medical examinations of his body revealed that he had been taking amphetamines to give him extra energy for the long rides. Since this energy was not extra, but only borrowed, he literally 'burnt himself out' in the heat of the race. Despite this serious incident, cyclists continue to be tempted to take **stimulants** and many riders in the 1998 Tour de France were disqualified after failing drugs tests.

Simpson's death showed how 'ordinary' amphetamines could be lethal. Today the problem is even more complex. Powerful derivatives of amphetamines, such as 'meth' and 'ice', have led to a dramatic increase in public-health responsibility where these drugs are commonly used. Ice, with its terrible **addictive** qualities and easy scope for overdosing, has been a major cause for concern in the late 1990s. The use of ice lies behind a particularly alarming statistic: amphetamine-related emergency hospital admissions rose 460 per cent from 1985 to 1994 in California alone. This version of amphetamines is far less common in Britain, but many drugs have the tendency to blossom almost overnight, bringing the immediate consequences with them.

Needle sharing

Injecting amphetamines leads to another serious risk which health authorities have been trying to control. Drug users who inject are tempted to share needles. This brings terrible dangers of spreading the **HIV** infection, which can lead to the deadly disease AIDS. Many health authorities and drugs counselling centres operate 'needle exchange' schemes whereby drug users can dispose of used needles in exchange for new, clean ones. Getting these people off drugs is considered secondary to preventing the spread of a fatal infection through the community.

Legal matters

Under the terms of the Medicines Act in the UK, all amphetamines and similar **stimulants** are 'prescription only' drugs. This means that they can only be supplied by a pharmacist working from a registered pharmacy on presentation of a doctor's prescription. Despite the well-known side-effects of amphetamines, their legitimate medical uses mean that doctors can still prescribe them and patients can legally possess them on prescription.

Other circumstances of amphetamine production and possession are strictly illegal. The unauthorized production, supply or possession of amphetamines is an offence under the law. The Misuse of Drugs Act (see panel) classifies illegal drugs and sets the punishments for offences. In the UK when someone is caught with illegal drugs the police must take one of the following actions. They can either issue a Reprimand or a Warning to 10-17 year olds, or if the person is over 17 they can issue an Adult Caution. Or the police can decide to charge the person with an offence.

The sentence served by someone convicted of possessing amphetamines depends on the person's age. Up to the age of 17, people are tried in a young offenders' court, which can give a maximum sentence of one year in a young offenders' institution. People who are 18 or older go through the **magistrates' courts** which can impose longer sentences (up to five years for possession), although until someone is 21 they still serve the time in a young offenders' institution.

In Australia, it is illegal to possess, manufacture, supply, import or trade amphetamines. Penalties range from $2,000 and/or two years in prison to a $500,000 fine and/or life imprisonment.

The Misuse of Drugs Act

The Misuse of Drugs Act 1971 divides drugs into three classes and gives guidelines for penalties. Class A drugs, which include cocaine, crack, heroin and LSD, are considered most serious and the penalty for supply can be life imprisonment. If amphetamines have been prepared for **injection**, they become part of this classification. Otherwise, amphetamines and cannabis are considered Class B drugs, which carry up to a fourteen-year prison sentence for supply. Supplying some drugs such as steroids and tranquillizers – although they are in the least serious category (Class C) – can still lead to a criminal record or a prison sentence and fine.

A haul of illegal amphetamines is displayed in a police headquarters. Penalties for dealing in the drug are severe.

Life with amphetamines

Young people who take amphetamines to feel 'high' follow a pattern similar to that of heavy drinking, even though the results are very different. It is quite common for such people to **binge**, taking amphetamines steadily for two to three days, and then 'come down' for a slightly longer period. For many people the binge period is the weekend, and the work or school week begins with a prolonged 'down' phase.

During this time the user's body tries to catch up with the energy that it lost while the amphetamines were having their effect. If the person is not a regular user, these effects will be confined to a general sense of being washed out. However, it is also common for occasional users to experience mood swings, anger and confusion the day after taking amphetamines. These effects usually pass – for the occasional user – and some of the physical feelings represent the body's need to replenish essential nutrients. Eating a lot more than normal is one way of addressing this problem and many occasional users have this urge anyway.

Spiralling network

Young people often hear the chorus 'but it could lead to other drugs', usually levelled at use of cannabis or other drugs that have a reputation for being safe. Amphetamines present just such a danger, and many regular users admit that they do form only part of a tapestry of drug use and **dependence**. Perhaps the most common drugs used in conjunction with amphetamines are alcohol and **barbiturates**. The reason for this is simple. Alcohol seems to offer the chance to relieve the sense of depression that accompanies an amphetamine hangover; also – like barbiturates – it seems to take the edge off the jitters and restlessness.

Another reason for this multiple drug use is that the mind becomes accustomed to taking a drug to change the mood. The same **neurons** that remember the pleasurable effects of amphetamines soon come to expect a hangover 'cure' in the form of a mood-relaxer.

A way of life

This pattern of rapid 'high', leading to an inevitable 'low', followed by another drug-induced 'calm' can sometimes occur among occasional users if the amounts of amphetamines taken were high. It is more commonly a pattern of behaviour among long-term amphetamine users, whose regular use of the drugs has built up a **tolerance** that leads to the need for higher doses. These are the users whose lifestyle changes the most, and their greater involvement with amphetamines – and the spin-offs – puts them firmly within the 'drug culture'.

Life with amphetamines

Within this world of drugs, one of the most important influences on behaviour is word of mouth. Long-term, high-dose amphetamine users have usually long since abandoned the circle of friends who might have steered them away from their spiralling use of drugs. Instead, they turn to more experienced drug users who can advise them on the best way to 'cheat the system' – in this case the body's natural system – and often with profoundly damaging consequences.

Coded messages

Regular amphetamine users often feel themselves to be part of a 'select few' who live life on the line. Over the years popular music has given them some sense of 'belonging', as they identify with the coded messages linked to the names of bands or their lyrics. In the 1980s, the British band Dexy's Midnight Runners seemed to promote a type of amphetamines (dexies). The word 'amphetamine' itself leads off the lyrics of 'Annie Dog' by the Smashing Pumpkins and the website of the band Everclear is entitled simply 'amphetamine'.

A high-profile addict

It takes a great deal of moral courage to face up to **addiction** – and even more to publicize the effects that it has had. One such person is Kitty Dukakis, the wife of US presidential candidate Michael Dukakis. During her husband's gruelling 1988 campaign she spoke often about her own 26-year addiction to amphetamine pills, which started when she took them as a dieting aid. Her own candid admissions about the pain that this addiction had caused her and her family helped bring the issue of drug addiction to the public eye. It also showed that such addiction knows no boundaries – of gender, wealth or social standing.

In February 1989 Mrs Dukakis was admitted to a clinic for treatment of an alcohol-**dependence** problem. Again it was her wish that her husband 'come clean' about this issue. Kitty Dukakis's fight against such **addictive** behaviour also pointed out the problems discussed elsewhere on these pages – that of **cross-dependency**. Like so many other regular amphetamine users, she had turned to alcohol as a 'solution'. This move led to yet more problems, which she could only face by abandoning any mood-altering drugs.

Kitty Dukakis, wife of US presidential candidate Michael Dukakis, has overcome her own amphetamine addiction and now talks openly about it.

Treatment and counselling

With amphetamines, as with most other drugs that produce
dependence, the first step towards effective treatment must really come
from the drug user. Drug therapists and counsellors recognize this fact
and make it easier for such a decision to be taken by asking the
following six questions about 'speed' (amphetamines):

- Do you use speed regularly?
- Do you think about how and when you are going to use
  speed again?
- Is your work or school performance affected by your drug use?
- Are you having problems with family and friends?
- Do you spend more on speed than you can afford?
- Do you use other drugs in addition to speed?

A 'yes' to any one of these questions suggests that a person should
think about the way they view speed and its effect on their life.
Dealing with amphetamines involves a two-pronged approach. The
more immediate aim is a medical one – overcoming the direct
problems associated with a particular dose. Everyone should be aware
of what the obvious symptoms are. Some immediate responses are
outlined in the section on 'first aid' on page 49.

The role of counsellors

Therapists and counsellors confront the more long-term problem of
amphetamine use, and its effects on the user. Many users lead chaotic
lives, which means that they are less likely to stick to appointment
times, meet schedules set out by clinics and so on.

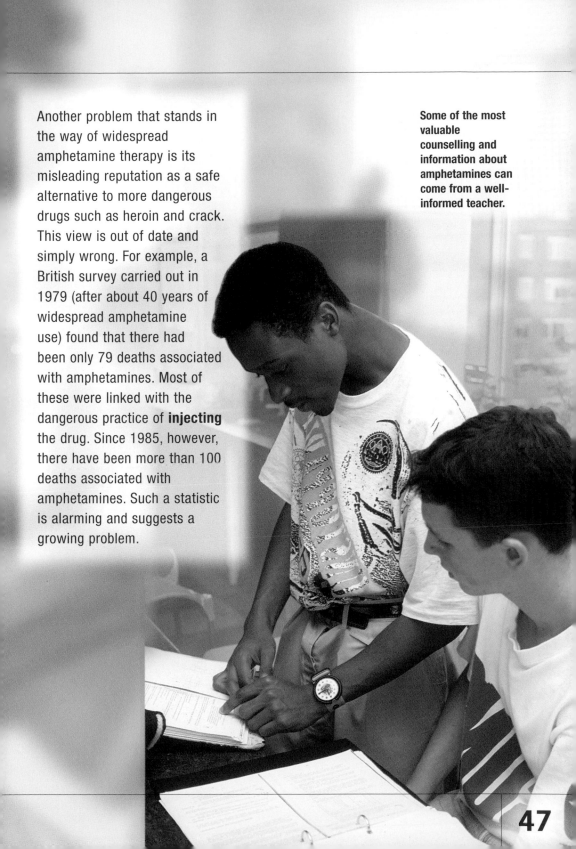

Another problem that stands in the way of widespread amphetamine therapy is its misleading reputation as a safe alternative to more dangerous drugs such as heroin and crack. This view is out of date and simply wrong. For example, a British survey carried out in 1979 (after about 40 years of widespread amphetamine use) found that there had been only 79 deaths associated with amphetamines. Most of these were linked with the dangerous practice of **injecting** the drug. Since 1985, however, there have been more than 100 deaths associated with amphetamines. Such a statistic is alarming and suggests a growing problem.

Some of the most valuable counselling and information about amphetamines can come from a well-informed teacher.

Treatment and counselling

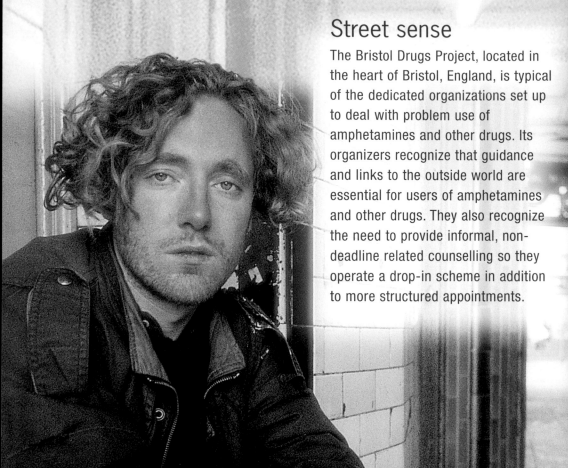

Street sense

The Bristol Drugs Project, located in the heart of Bristol, England, is typical of the dedicated organizations set up to deal with problem use of amphetamines and other drugs. Its organizers recognize that guidance and links to the outside world are essential for users of amphetamines and other drugs. They also recognize the need to provide informal, non-deadline related counselling so they operate a drop-in scheme in addition to more structured appointments.

❝We're hearing from young people and street drugs workers that (speed) has become the drug that replaces ecstasy when ecstasy becomes boring or they've had a bad experience with it. What is more worrying is that we are hearing that people are using amphetamine base which is a much stronger form of the drug.❞

(Sally Murray of the Kaleidoscope Project, Kingston-upon-Thames, UK)

Justin Mason, youth co-ordinator of the Bristol Drugs Project, is experienced with dealing with many areas of drug problems. 'There's a steady flow of people coming through the doors here. Some have the sense to see that they're playing with their minds and bodies with speed – and they might take immediate action. Others might drop in, maybe just the once. We can only hope that the message got through to some degree and that they'll be able to sort themselves out.'

Information, support and advice covers treatment schemes and counselling as well as referrals to other agencies if need be. 'We're often the only source of unbiased information that a user gets,' Julian points out. 'We are also aware of the problems associated with **injecting** speed and other drugs. Our needle exchange policy recognizes the reality that injectors are out there. For them, the exchange is one way to stay a little bit safer. The real steps to safety, though, need to come from the users themselves.

First aid

Although amphetamines are often taken in crowded venues such as raves or music festivals, people can often miss the signs that someone near them is having a bad drugs experience. The following is basic advice for dealing with such an emergency.

If the user feels tense or anxious:

- calm them down and reassure them that everything is OK
- talk quietly and explain that the panicky feeling will gradually go
- keep them away from loud noises and bright lights
- encourage them to breath slowly and deeply to avoid **hyperventilation**.

Taking amphetamines, especially in crowded surroundings, often leads to overheating and dehydration. The warning signs are:

- cramps in the legs, arms and back
- failure to sweat
- headaches, dizziness and vomiting
- suddenly feeling very tired and even fainting
- feeling like urinating, but not being able to do much.

If someone has overheated, then:

- move them to a cooler area and remove any excess clothing
- encourage them to drink non-alcoholic fluids
- call an ambulance if the problem continues, and tell the ambulance crew what you have done.

People to talk to

There are very few drugs that people begin taking on their own, for private recreation. More often, people get 'high' or 'buzzed' in the company of others. This is certainly true for young people – and for amphetamines. While amphetamines can be abused in a number of settings, including by solitary users for losing weight or simply staying awake, they are usually taken by users in groups. Word of mouth – both about what it's like being high and how 'safe' and uplifting amphetamines are meant to be – form the basis of many people's introduction to the drug. This type of **peer pressure** is not helpful, but it is a strong and persuasive force.

Other voices

There are people who can put amphetamines in a different perspective, either by giving first-hand accounts of their own experiences with the drug or by outlining the clear dangers of amphetamine use. Parents and older family members are usually the best people to turn to first. However, the teenage years are often the period when young people feel that they have least in common with their parents. Even sympathetic teachers and others in authority locally might seem too close to home.

The UK has a wide range of telephone contacts – many of them free of charge and most of them anonymous – where young people can find out more about how amphetamines are affecting them. Many of the organizations listed in the Information and advice section (pages 52–53) are specialist phone lines. They provide such a telephone service, or they can suggest local agencies throughout the UK.

Others are geared specifically to queries coming from younger people; they are listed separately on these pages. Whether you approach one of these organizations, or a family member, a youth leader or teacher, the important thing is to be able to talk – and listen – freely about amphetamine concerns. Sharing a problem or worry is the first step to solving it.

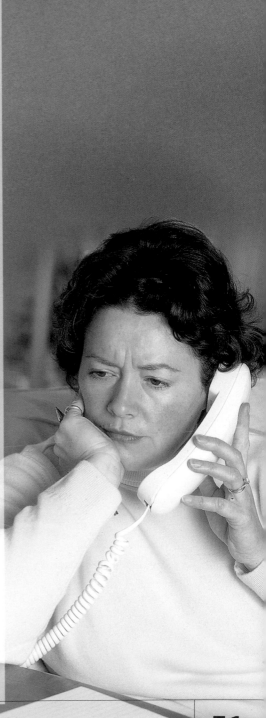

Information and advice

The UK is well served by organizations providing advice, counselling and other information relating to drug use. All of the contacts listed on these pages are helpful springboards for obtaining such advice or for providing confidential information over the telephone or by post.

Drug awareness contacts

ADFAM NATIONAL,
Tel: 020 7928 8900
This is a national (UK) hotline for the friends and families of drug users. It provides confidential support and information.

British Association for Counselling (BAC),
1 Regent Place, Rugby CV21 2PJ
www.bac.co.uk
The BAC has an extensive directory of counselling services relating to drugs and other issues throughout the UK. Enquiries are by post only. Enclose an SAE for a list of counsellors in your area.

ISDD (Institute for the Study of Drug Dependence), Waterbridge House,
32–36 Loman Street, London SE1 0EE
Tel: 020 7928 1211   www.bac.co.uk
The ISDD has the largest drugs reference library in Europe and provides leaflets and other publications. SCODA (Standing Committee on Drug Abuse) is located at the same address (tel: 020 7928 9500) and is one of the best UK contacts for information on drugs.

National Drugs Helpline,
Tel: 0800 776 600
The Helpline provides a freephone telephone contact for all aspects of drug use and has a database covering all of the British Isles for further information about specific drugs or regional information.

Release, Tel: 020 7603 8654
www.release.org.uk
Release operates a 24-hour helpline which provides advice on drug use and legal issues surrounding the subject.

Youth Access, 1A Taylors Yard, 67
Alderbrook Road, London SW12 8AD
Tel: 020 8772 9900
Youth Access is an organization which refers young people to their local counselling service. It has a database of approximately 350 such services throughout the UK.

Contacts in the United States

Child Welfare League of America, 440
First Street NW, Washington, DC 20001
Tel: 202/638-2952
www.cwla.org
The Child Welfare League of America, based in Washington, provides useful contacts across the country in most areas relating to young people's problems, many of them related to drug involvement.

DARE America, PO Box 775, Dumfries, VA 22026, Tel: 703/860-3273
www.dare-america.com
Drug Abuse Resistance and Education (DARE) America is a national organization that links law-enforcement and educational resources to provide up-to-date and comprehensive information about all aspects of drug use.

Youth Power, 300 Lakeside Drive, Oakland, CA 94612
Tel: 510/451-6666, ext. 24
Youth Power is a nationwide organization involved in widening awareness of drug-related problems. It sponsors clubs and local affiliates across the country in an effort to help young people make their own sensible choices about drugs, and to work against the negative effects of peer pressure.

Contacts in Australia

ADCA, PO Box 269, Woden, ACT 2606
www.adca.org.au
The Alcohol and other Drug Council of Australia (ADCA), based in the Capital Territory, gives an overview of drug awareness organizations in Australia. Most of their work is carried out over the Internet but the postal address provides a useful link for those who are not 'on-line'.

Australian Drug Foundation, 409 King Street, West Melbourne, VIC 3003
Tel: 03 9278 8100 www.adf.org.au
The Australian Drug Foundation (ADF) has a wide range of information on all aspects of drugs, their effects and the legal position in Australia. It also provides handy links to state- and local-based drug organizations.

Centre for Education and Information on Drugs and Alcohol, Private Mail Bag 6, Rozelle, NSW 2039
Tel: 02 9818 0401   www.ceida.net.au
The Centre for Education and Information on Drugs and Alcohol is the ideal contact for information on drug programmes throughout Australia. It also has one of the most extensive libraries on drug-related subjects in the world.

Further reading

Buzzed, by Cynthia Kuhn, Scott Swartzwelder and Wilkie Wilson; New York and London: W.W. Norton and Company, 1998

Drugs, by Anita Naik, part of Wise Guides Series; London: Hodder Children's Books, 1997

Drugs: the Facts, HEA leaflet; London: Health Education Authority, 1997

Drugs Wise, by Melanie McFadyean; Cambridge: Icon books, 1997

Taking Drugs Seriously, A Parent's Guide to Young People's Drug Use, by Julian Cohen and James Kay; London: Thorsons, 1994

The Score: Facts about Drugs, HEA leaflet; London: Health Education Authority, 1998

Glossary

acrid
having a sharp or bitter taste

acronym
an abbreviation formed by taking the first letters of words in a long phrase

addiction
the need to take something such as a drug

addictive
something that causes addiction or the behaviour of someone with an addiction

adrenaline
a natural substance in the body that is produced to respond to fear, anxiety or attack

Attention Deficit Disorder
a learning difficulty linked to an inability to concentrate on anything for very long

auditory
relating to hearing

barbiturates
drugs that calm the body down

Beat Generation
a name given to a group of writers and artists in the 1950s who rejected formal society and also experimented with drugs

binge
to take large amounts of something, such as a drug, at irregular intervals

black market
the illegal trade in something, such as drugs

compound
made up of two or more chemical substances

compulsive
driven to perform certain actions, often with no sense of control

cross-dependence
the dependence on a second drug initially taken to help deal with dependence on another drug

deficiencies
the dangerous lack of certain essential substances such as nutrients

dependence
the physical or psychological craving for something

dilate
to widen

dopamine
a chemical substance in the brain that regulates movement and emotion

euphoria
a sense that everything is wonderful

exhilaration
a condition or feeling of being invigorated or stimulated

freebase
a purified version of a drug, which is exceptionally powerful

hallucinations
images that people think they see, but which are not really there

HIV
Human Immunodeficiency Virus, which is linked with the disease AIDS

hyperventilation
breathing rapidly and deeply which causes someone to faint

inject
to take a drug by inserting fluid into the body through a needle

intravenous
taking a drug into a vein by injecting it

legislation
laws about a certain subject

lethargy
a powerful sense of tiredness, often coupled
with depression

magistrates' court
a court that deals with legal cases involving
relatively minor crimes

narcolepsy
a condition characterized by frequent and
uncontrollable periods of deep sleep

neurons
cells that form the basis of the nervous system

palpitations
to beat with great rapidity

paranoia
a sense that everyone is out to get you, or to
criticize your behaviour or actions

peer pressure
the impulse to do something because everyone
close to you is telling you to do it

pharmaceutical
chemical, used in a medical sense

prevalence
how widespread something is

psychological
relating to the mind and behaviour

psychosis
a mental condition in which a person loses
contact with reality

quotas
limits on quantities of something

recreational
with drugs, using them for pleasure rather than
for any medical reason

rehabilitation
returning to normal health

samurai
the name of the traditional warrior class in
Japan, which had a complex code of honour

Second World War
the war (1939–1945) between Germany, Japan
and their allies against Britain, the United
States and their allies

snort
to inhale a drug through the nostrils

stimulant
something that makes the body or the mind
work harder

strychnine
a colourless poison that in small doses works
as a stimulant

synthesize
to create by artificial means

tolerance
the way which the body learns to accept or
expect more of a substance

trade-name
the legal name of a product, which can only be
used by the company that makes it

withdrawal
negative physical effects of giving up a
substance

Index